RUNNING THROUGH THE THISTLES

terminating a ministerial
relationship with a parish

Roy M. Oswald

An Alban Institute Book
ROWMAN & LITTLEFIELD
Lanham • Boulder • New York • Toronto • Plymouth, UK

First Rowman & Littlefield paperback edition 2014

Published by Rowman & Littlefield
4501 Forbes Blvd, Suite 200, Lanham, MD 20706
www.rowman.com

10 Thornbury Road, Plymouth PL6 7PP, United Kingdom

Library of Congress Cataloging-in-Publication Data Available

ISBN 13: 978-1-56699-004-2 (pbk: alk. paper)

♾™ The paper used in this publication meets the minimum requirements of American National Standard for Information Sciences—Permanence of Paper for Printed Library Materials, ANSI/NISO Z39.48-1992.

Printed in the United States of America

Preface

For me this was an unusually helpful paper. But not the first
time around. I resisted its insights. It is packed full of un-
settling descriptions of what we do to our dear friends, and some
enemies, when we terminate relationships in an atmosphere of
avoidance and denial. I just didn't want to deal with these memories at that moment.

Because I was asked to write a preface I had to read it again,
and a third time. Each time it forced me to wrestle with some insights about my own style of leaving. These were situations I
preferred to forget. I've kept them buried for many years.

But gradually Roy Oswald's ability to clarify these sensitive
issues encouraged me to see that however badly I felt about certain past leavings I could intentionally change my pattern for
future leavings. His paper suggests ways to bring about these
changes.

Particularly convincing was Oswald's often made point that not
to deal openly and honestly with one's own grief at leaving results in "tragic disregard for the emotional needs of congregations, staff and friends involved. This results in feelings of
abandonment, betrayal, frustration and artificiality."

. Well, if that's what I have done to people by "stealing off
in the night," believing this was the kindest way to go, I must
reconsider my pattern of leaving. I thought such departures
were painful only to me. Now he tells me--and I am slowly coming to agree with him--that this is a cruel thing to do to other
people as well. If my dear friends, whom I abandon, and I all
suffer, then my old grief pattern demands a complete overhaul.

I am sure others who read this piece will examine their style
of leaving just as I did. And it could make quite a difference
in the way scores of people who are close to us set about to re-
work their lives after we have left them.

Granger E. Westberg
President,
Wholistic Health Centers, Inc.

RUNNING THROUGH THE THISTLES:

Terminating a Ministerial Relationship
with a Parish

*From the time I announced my resignation
at St. Margaret's through my final Sunday
six weeks later, the comparisons of terminating with a parish and dying occurred
to me often. While the congregation went
through emotions analogous to having a
significant person die, my emotions were
those of the person dying.*

*Throughout the time I felt a mixture
of emotions. I felt sadness at the pros-
pect of separating my life from the lives
of many who had been significant persons
for me and at separating from a community
which had been nurturing for me. I felt
a mixture of anticipation for a new adventure and some fear of the unknown.*

*Then there were the more down to earth
feelings that came as I ended relationships with people -- trying to articulate
what our relationship had been and strug-
gling to face the fact that they would be
ended or at least changed in a most significant way. At first I wanted to have
some control over what happened in the
parish after I left. I acted some of
this out and finally realized that I must
let go of this influence in order for me
to leave. Finally there was a celebration of what my relationship had been
with the parish (like a funeral with me
present to hear the eulogies) and this
was good. It left me feeling ready to
leave and start a new adventure.*

*The comparisons with dying were many --
it takes conscious effort and courage to
face what needs to be done. Some matters
I did not face but hopefully the experience did prepare me for better "dyings"
along the way henceforth.*

Parke Street

Elisabeth Kubler-Ross describes death
as the "Final Stage of Growth."[1] Death
provides us with that final opportunity

to come to terms with our relationships,
our values, our lives. Similarly, the
process of grieving the death of a loved
one, if approached from a stance of openness and vulnerability, provides a growth
opportunity. In death and in grief, we
do not so much need protection from painful experience as we need the boldness to
face it. If we choose love, we must also
have the courage to grieve.

All of the above, if true for death,
is true in microcosm when we terminate
our relationship with a parish. The same
opportunities for learning and growth as
well as the same temptations for avoidance
and denial are present. All depends upon
our approach and style.

There is one additional powerpacked
insight available to us as we terminate
our relationship with a parish. The manner and style in which we close out that
ministry will be very similar to the way
in which we will die. As we observe ourselves in the context of a ministerial
closure we may ask ourselves, "Is this
the manner in which I want to die?" If
not, then some intentional things need to
be done on our part to change that.

In the past few years, we as clergy
have learned much about the death and dying process. We need to take this insight,
this skill and understanding, and apply
it to ourselves and our congregations as
we make the transition to another setting.

We belong to a death-denying culture.
Ernest Becker has so poignantly illustrated
that for us in his book The Denial of
Death. As we encounter energy parishioners
expend in denying their death or the death
of loved ones, so also we need to look
at our own death-denying tendencies as we
seek to gain closure on a ministry in a
parish.

Parke Street was aware of this when
he wrote down his reflections upon leaving

*Written for the Washington Episcopal
Clergy Association newsletter. Parke
Street is now Rector, St. Augustine's
Episcopal Church, Washington, D.C.

[1]Death, The Final Stage of Growth, Elisabeth Kubler-Ross, Prentice-Hall, Inc.,
Englewood Cliffs, N.J., 1975.

St. Margaret's parish. He was in touch with his parish's need to grieve over his leaving. He was in touch with his own pain at terminating that relationship. And he was able to connect that experience with future "dying" he would have to do.

Running Through the Thistles

When I was a young boy, age six, growing up in rural Saskatchewan, my two older brothers and I would often decide to walk home from school over the fields, rather than along the road. It was shorter, to be sure, but occasionally we would come upon enormous thistle patches. I cannot remember seeing anything like it since, but those thistle patches sometimes used to extend for a half mile or more. In places the prickly patches would be 50 feet to 100 feet wide -- in other places 10 to 20 feet. The rest of the field, lying fallow in summer, was tilled soil. We rarely wore shoes to school in the summertime, hence our dilemma: how to cross these thistle patches in bare feet. We did have the choice of walking around them, but, since it was the end of the day, we were all tired and hungry. We were anxious to get home. Mother usually had a snack treat for us to tide us over 'till supper. To walk around the patch would take us way out of our way. The other option was to back up and run through the narrowest part at full speed. Being the youngest -- with the least speed and the smallest leg span -- I always objected. I was usually over-ruled, however, by my two other brothers, who would then each take me by one hand and run me through the thistle patch.

I can still vividly remember the experience: running full speed in bare feet across 20 feet of prickly thistles, yelping in pain all the way through. When the three of us reached the black soil on the other side, we would immediately hit the dirt and start pulling out the few thistle ends that stuck in our feet. "I had four briars get me -- how many did you get?" was a sample of our post agony conversation.

For me this story illustrates how some pastors approach their termination periods. They rightly assume that there will be pain involved, so their approach is to run through it as fast as they can.

This kind of manic behavior at the closure of a ministry does have certain advantages -- but there is a price to pay as well. Beyond this, it is clearly a death denying approach to closing out one's life in one place.

The advantage of running full speed through the closure of a ministry is that of giving short shrift to the most painful parts of that experience. As I watch clergy and army chaplains attempt this type of exit, I'm reminded of the time in my first parish when I needed to catch an airplane for a conference yet had to pay a quick visit to some of my parishioners at the hospital before I left. I realized afterwards that I had not really listened to where those people were nor shared where I was. I wanted to make an appearance -- say a quick prayer over the sick person -- and run to catch my plane.

That's the tenor and quality of the farewells of church professionals who try to run through their termination experiences.

The problem is this approach usually backfires. This was my style in leaving my first parish, and it did for me. As in running through the thistles, we always end up with briars in our feet on the other side. The briars are the powerful emotions that we have not dealt with. It's impossible to stuff powerful feelings down inside, paint a smile on our face, and come out the other side feeling whole or good about ourselves.

This is where termination of a ministry is quite unlike the experience of our own death. Following the closing out of a ministry, we continue to live, and we have to cope with unexpressed feelings and emotions. Psychological studies have given us ample evidence that repression usually does not work very well. Those repressed emotions will emerge somehow -- possibly in unexpected ways that make us more like victims than actors in life. It is very difficult, if not impossible, to emerge at the other side of a death denying termination as a whole person. This in turn makes a wholesome, life-giving ministry with new people equally impossible.

The Sponge Approach

An alternate approach is to try to be open and receptive to the feelings of parishioners at the time of termination. This is an attempt to be a good Rogerian listener throughout the termination period. Clergy who attempt this type of closure usually become more and more depressed and increasingly more fatigued. There is a passivity to it that is life draining. As opposed to the manic behavior of a thistle runner, these folks end up sleeping their way through the farewell period.

It's hard work sitting on one's own grief, hence the depression and fatigue. What's required to break out of this is to become open and candid with others about what we're going through emotionally and spiritually, in addition to being open and receptive to where others are.

Once again we can take a lesson from those who have completed much research on the death and dying process. To quote from Mwalimu Imara in Death, The Final Stage of Growth: "to be transformed, dying patients must be committed to 1) achieving a sense of their own identity through experiencing their own ongoing awareness of 'original experience,' 2) committing themselves to a mutual dialogue about that experience with significant other people."

We do need to be clearly in touch with our own feelings and emotions throughout a ministerial closure. Second, we need to discover ways in which we can be open to significant others about those things and be fully present as they try to be open and candid with us.

Alban Institute Research

The Alban Institute got into the study of clergy termination styles through work with its Pastorate Start Up Project. In that project we attempted to get some practical handles on the entire clergy transition process. It became clear to us rather early that the grief process of clergy and congregations had direct relevance to the subsequent start up process. We coined the phrase "termination emotions" to cover that dimension of life.

We discovered that when congregations, as total entities, had not experienced a good termination process they carried that unresolved work with them when new pastoral leadership arrived on the scene. There were times when the grief over a former long-time pastor rendered a congregation incapable of accepting new pastoral leadership. In these cases, the new pastor merely became an "Interim Pastor" and left in frustration, hurt and disappointment after a few years. In other situations, congregational leaders appeared to have great difficulty with sound decision-making processes at the time of ministerial selection. We have come to recognize that difficulty with decisions can be a symptom of a congregation in grief.

In still other circumstances we encountered cases of clergy who had to listen to endless stories of the former pastor for a year or more. It's our sense of things that congregational members who do not have the opportunity to express their grief directly to the departing clergyperson will need to express those sentiments somewhere. The new pastor is the most likely candidate.

The other side of our research led us to discover clergy who arrived in their new pastorate carrying with them many unresolved feelings about leaving their last situation. The same may be true, possibly more so, for their spouses and children. This leads to feelings of depression and discouragement. They find it hard to become energized with their new ministry. Fatigue and despondency characterize their start up period. All signs point to their having denied and avoided their grief in their former location.

Some clergy end up confusing their grief reaction at leaving with their decision to accept a call elsewhere. (This is most prevalent in non-appointive systems, where clergy themselves must decide to move or stay when another parish calls them.) Part of our research involved simply asking clergy to log their experience from termination to start up. Listen to the account of a Lutheran pastor's ambivalence once he had accepted a call elsewhere.

May 22. Today is Tuesday. Last Sunday I resigned. I was nervous. Yesterday and today I am depressed about the whole thing. I feel like having a fit. Psychologically I know it is an aftereffect. I know this, but this is how I feel.

4

*Everything looks so green and beautiful
and attractive here all of a sudden. How
can that be!*

*Some of my pastor friends are envious
of our move. For 2¢ I will give them
the whole struggle. I dread this move.
Yet, I get excited realizing the great
benefits that will come to this church --
and to our new church.*

*Sometimes I think this whole business
has been of the devil. But then, how
many times have we prayed and prayed for
guidance? And prayed that the Lord would
protect us from the devil, and encompass
us so that Satan would be fenced out of
this decision.*

*If I have been misled by the devil, I
am in a bad way, because then I have been
unable to discern God's will. How shall
one know what the will of God is? But why
this constant struggle? Does the devil not
want me at my new parish? Do I have such
potential to work with my brothers and sis-
ters there that the devil would harass me
like this? Or is God saying "no" and I
failed to listen? Or is God saying "yes,"
and the devil harassing me? Is all this
odd or God?*

*May 27. Yesterday and the day before
were just terrible. In fact I suggested
to Bernell (wife) we call off the whole
venture! My feelings and desire to stay
here were so strong. So many good things
seem to be happening just now.... People
are visiting who are expressing sadness
and regret at my leaving. And others have
said, "You have everything going for you."
That has caused me to look around and reflect again.**

How well each of us can empathize with
the "dark night of the soul" that this
pastor is going through. As grief over-
whelms us, our isolation and loneliness
increase. We continue to confuse our
grief with whether or not we made the right
decision.

Research with the USA Army Chaplains Board

As part of a contract to work with the
Chaplains Board to offer assistance to
its chaplains in transition, a team of
four of us, three Army chaplains from

---

*Personal Diary, Orval K. Moren, Summer
1974 to 1977.

other bases and myself, visited an Army
base in the U.S. to study the termination styles of seven Army chaplains.
These chaplains either had moved to new
assignments or were about to move in a matter of weeks. The research team carried
out extensive interviews with parishioners
and Army personnel who had firsthand con-
tact with these chaplains.

The following were our basic assumptions
when we began that work:

1) Army chaplains have a variety of
styles of terminating their ministries
as they move from one assignment to another.

2) Each chaplain's termination style
remains basically the same throughout his
career as a chaplain.

3) Some of these styles serve to enhance the ministry of these chaplains,
bringing a period of service to a meaningful conclusion.

4) Other styles of disengaging serve
only to diminish the overall effectiveness
of a period of ministry, bringing it to an
unsatisfactory conclusion.

5) Army chaplains could be greatly as-
sisted during their termination periods if
they had a clear vision of the variety of
exiting styles and the resultant consequences connected with each.

Insights and Conclusions by the Research Team

Of the seven chaplains studied, it was the
research team's conclusion that only two
had a termination style that enhanced
their ministry and left people with a positive feeling about their closure process.
The team isolated the following character-
istics of the two chaplains who exhibited
an effective closure style.

- The departing chaplains were perceived as being authentic and genuine
throughout the process.

- They remained conscientious about
their assignments until the very end.

- Both maintained an informal posture
with those close to them.

- They tried to take into consideration
all groups they were involved with during
their departure: their families, their
friends, the command structure, their congregations.

- They accepted the fact that the future
ministry of their situations belonged to

someone else, hence worked to develop an acceptable climate for this new person.

- Both remained open to personal invitations into people's homes, thus placing themselves in situations where people could work through their feelings about their termination.

A strong feature of one of the chaplain's styles was his taking control of his own termination process. He planned and executed the whole procedure with the help of some friends. To the credit of the second chaplain, even though he requested no formal farewell occasion be planned for him, he consented to one because he became convinced that his parishioners needed an opportunity to do this for him.

Of the five remaining chaplains, the research team concluded that their termination manner and style detracted from and diminished what appeared to be a positive ministry with people. For the most part, people were left with a bad taste in their mouths over the way they took their leave, or parishioners were left confused by the chaplain's departure, wondering whether he really cared for them in the first place.

The following quotes from those we interviewed tell their own story.

"He had a hard time being straight with folks, especially those in authority, hence never dealt openly and honestly with what he was going through for his last month and a half."

"He received a bad review from a commanding officer. This seemed to affect his termination style. He was like a boy caught with his hand in the cookie jar. He would act sheepish and philosophical about his situation. He accepted his judgment. He avoided dealing with his commanding officer. He asked to be moved from the people in his battalion for the last six weeks (avoidance)."

"He was a control taking person, attempting to control others and the situation most of the time. Towards the end he had difficulty letting go. He tried to leave everything in tip top shape even if it meant having to manipulate people in order

to do it. Even though he is an emotional person, he was not able to open up. He hated farewells. That's why I guess he just slipped away into the night."

"Right up until the very end, he acted as though he wasn't even leaving. He always was a competitive person. I believe this really blocked him from any kind of honest closure with his peers. On the last day there were some very quick 'good byes' and he ran out the door."

"He shared the fact of his termination with parishioners but did not share his inner feelings with them. He tried hard to see that the work he had started would continue. His termination at the end was hectic - abrupt - anxious."

"His departure was like a one man show - abrupt."

"He's what we call a bridge cutter."

"He used the garbage disposal method of dropping people. He even dropped his personal friends."

"Termination was hurried -- this was a future oriented guy. Things in the office were neat, tidy and in order. He even wrote a job profile for his successor."

From the perspective of the research team, the most popular model of termination among chaplains to be observed is:
- Bite the Bullet (deny and avoid dealing with personal feelings)
- Don't allow your emotions to show
- Put up with whatever type of event others plan for you at your departure
- Steal off into the night.

To the credit of the Chaplains Corps, there were the earlier mentioned notable exceptions to this termination style. The chaplains who seem to fare better in the opinions of those interviewed were those who were much more people-oriented in their exit styles. Less appreciated were those who were more program-oriented (working hard up to the end to see that there was continuity of program) or self- or future-oriented (working to prepare themselves for the next assignment).

The following three diagrams illustrate how each person terminating can emphasize one of these three orientations more than the others. All three need some attention. We recommend diagram (1) as being more helpful and appropriate at the time of ministerial closure.

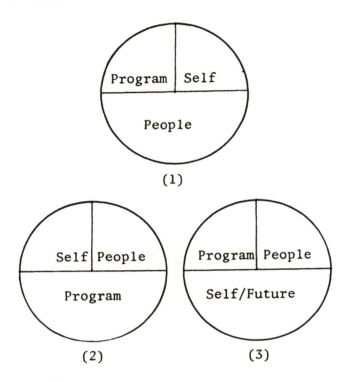

It's questionable, however, whether someone can become people-oriented at the conclusion of one's ministry if he/she hasn't been that way throughout that pastorate. It does, however, provide clergy with a brief road map of what style is best at termination.

In summing up our findings about the exit styles of Army chaplains, the team agreed upon the following conclusions:

1) Chaplains generally lack skill in knowing how to deal with the grief of leaving.

2) The current norms and rituals in the Army and the Chaplains Corps are usually used to avoid the acknowledgement of the deep feelings and emotional involvements that occur upon termination.

3) Refusal to deal with grief involves a tragic disregard for the emotional needs of congregations, staffs and friends involved. This results in feelings of abandonment, betrayal, frustration and artifi-ciality.

4) Where there is willingness to share feelings at one's termination, there is an experience of freedom and completeness. Following this experience:
   -People usually are not afraid to enter into other relationships
   -They are allowed to risk another close friendship.
This openness also builds a helpful climate for the successor.

5) If supervising chaplains or others trained and assigned to fulfill this duty on each Post would call in the chaplain terminating a ministry, the following options would be possible:
   - The one leaving would have an opportunity to discuss with another person the issues and emotions involved in his/her departure.
   - The individual could be invited to take control of his/her own termination process and plan for it.
   - The supervisor could encourage caring and emotional reality as part of this person's termination.

The research team felt that each supervising chaplain could make this part of his continuing ministry to those close to him. The Post chaplain could perform this function for supervising chaplains. There was general agreement that most chaplains could use some outside assistance at these times in their ministry.

Termination Tasks
My friend and colleague at the Alban Institute, John Fletcher, has recently been studying the institutional cost of caring for terminally ill patients. He is very clear that terminally ill people have four major tasks to perform when they discover they will die soon:

1) They need to take control of what remains of their life (as far as possible), with some help if necessary, as opposed to passively letting others dictate the way they will die.

2) They need to get their affairs in order (make a will if they haven't already done so, take care of loans, debts, etc.).

3) They need to let old grudges go. This implies dealing directly and candidly with those against whom they harbour resentment, anger, disappointment, etc.

4) They need to say "thank you" to the people for whom they feel gratitude.

When these four things are not occurring in the lives of terminally ill persons, John makes a strong case for its being the clergyperson's calling and function to assist these persons so these tasks are performed. It is not the job of doctors or nurses or funeral directors to see that these final developmental tasks are accomplished.

It is my perception that these four closure tasks are equally important for clergy as they resign from their parishes and begin their termination process.

I. Taking Control of the Situation

There is a real temptation to be passive and receptive once a resignation has been announced to the congregation. One feels helpless -- hence the tendency to render oneself helpless. It's important, however, to be quite intentional about the manner in which we gain closure on our ministries. We need to develop a plan of action, with an accompanying time schedule. Appropriate people need to be consulted about the plan, and it may be very helpful to hire a consultant to assist with this task. One way to begin might be to list those people who need special attention -- for example:

1) Who are the people who are going to need special time and attention because our relationship over time has been difficult and troubled?

2) Who are the special people with whom I want to visit personally to say "goodbye?"

3) Who are the people whom I, at least, want to call on the telephone before leaving?

4) Who are the people to whom I want to write a letter?

5) Which groups in the parish do I want to drop in on before leaving?

II. Getting Your Affairs in Order

The future ministry in this place no longer belongs to us. Others will need to come and do the job their way. We need to get things in order so that our successors are able to identify appropriate tasks for themselves. There are probably many business transactions that need to be taken care of prior to our leaving. Listing these and carrying them out before departing is important.

III. Letting Go of Old Grudges

It's time now to clean the slate. A good way to render ourselves disfunctional at the new place of ministry is to carry all the old grudges with us. If we excuse ourselves by protesting that it won't do any good anyway, we are mistaken. Even if the other person or persons do not respond as we hope, at least we have been clear and candid about our feelings and perceptions. We then no longer carry the complete burden of the problem with us.

I am not talking here about some irresponsible "dumping" on folks. The intent still is for resolution and reconciliation. We need to be ready and willing to risk being vulnerable for that to take place. Who knows? It may be that within the context of our leaving some forgiveness and reconciliation can take place.

IV. Saying "Thank You"

We need to say "thank you" to appropriate people. What is called for here is more than just "thanks." This task means being straight with people about our deeper feelings about them. This includes the sharing of our disappointments and frustrations as well as the positive feelings of love, affection, caring, etc. To some extent, the third and fourth tasks need to be combined as we deal with the people who have been significant to us in this ministry. Gaining closure with individuals calls for the two of us reviewing our total relationship, its good times and its bad times, acknowledging and celebrating both aspects of the friendship. For me, meaningful closure occurs when no aspect of the relationship is either denied or avoided at the time of departure.

V.

I would add one other item to this list. It has to do with being straight and clear about reasons for leaving. Time and again our research has surfaced a need members have to know that their pastor is not leaving because of something they did or failed to do. (If that is the pastor's reason for leaving, of course candor is called for.) We have discovered that lay people normally carry a lot of sadness and guilt when their pastor leaves. Their feelings of emptiness and loneliness are heightened by self-doubt. John Wyatt, Episcopal bishop of Spokane, tells us: "I've found it is a real relief to people when they are able to say that their departing minister has a more important job or he'll be getting more money. That assures them he is not leaving them because they are no good, and it also assures them, if they love him, that he is going to be in better shape than he is now."

Hiring a Consultant

I am not recommending in this monograph that you try to do all of this on your own. Let's admit to our humanness and vulnerability at the time of a ministerial closure. We have been with these people through the highs and lows of their lives. More than likely our pastorate can be characterized as a roller coaster. We've gone from birth and joy to death and tragedy with these folks -- sometimes within the same day. We have become inextricably tied into their lives. When it's time for us to leave, they can't be expected to be objective about it and neither can we. It's an excellent time to bring in a third party who can act as a midwife to the expressions of life that need to be voiced if wholeness is to occur on the other side of termination.

It's important that the outside resource person be consultant to both the congregation and the pastor during this closure period, but it's especially important that he/she work with you, the clergyperson. The consultant needs to work with you to help you ascertain how you're going to gain control of your termination and how you plan to leave this parish. A consultant is able to help you think through each step of your leave-taking and, more importantly, what the likely consequences of each of those steps might be. For example:

- How do you plan on communicating your resignation to the congregation?

- Who ought to help decide your timetable - how long to stay after your resignation? What process is appropriate for those decisions?

- What will consume the major part of your energy during the time that remains?

- Where will you get support to deal with your personal grief and anxiety? Where will your family get that support?

- What is your plan for saying "goodbye" to the people who have been meaningful to you during this pastorate?

- What are your plans for dealing with the people who have been problematic for your ministry here?

- What will you say to the congregation as a whole that will express both your joys and your disappointments during your sojourn with them...and how will you elicit their candid assessment of both your strengths and weaknesses as a pastor to them?

These and other questions you will think of suggest the ways in which a consultant can help you be more proactive and intentional about your closing out the pastorate. When our answers begin to sound more like avoidance and denial, the consultant can help us take a look at why we are doing that.

More importantly, however, the consultant can help you by being a sounding board for the deeper feelings you're experiencing at this time. If, for example, you end up having some powerful feelings of anger and hostility towards the congregation or a segment of it, it's best to be able to share that first with a trusted individual. That gives you the opportunity to get a sense of the weight and size of that feeling. An inappropriate or untimely expression of that anger may block meaningful dialogue. You can be more intentional about how much or what parts of that anger needs to be expressed and under what circumstances.

The consultant can also do some effective work with the congregation as a whole. One characteristic of a congregation in grief is difficulty in making appropriate meaningful decisions.

With some frequency, I've heard of clergy who had to receive a farewell gift or listen to a farewell speech by an individual who had been a "thorn in the flesh" during their ministry there. These clergy had some difficulty in being convinced that the words spoken were authentic. More than likely, the people who should have been presenting those gifts or giving those speeches were too overcome by grief to do so. An outside, objective resource person could possibly recognize this and offer to work with that situation.

Key to the consultant's work with the congregation is his/her ability to help a planning committee plan for a meaningful yet realistic celebration of the life you and this congregation have experienced together. A congregation overcome by grief may want to express only the positive side of the ministry that has just ended. That kind of farewell celebration oozes with saccharin speeches and comments. It's no wonder many folks hate farewells when they are often so unreal. They seem divorced from the actual life that was there.

Every ministry has had its ups and downs; its good times and its bad times. The farewell celebration needs to reflect the realism of this life that was shared. When this happens, people's humanness is affirmed and celebrated. People also feel as though their sensibilities and integrity have not been violated at such an event.

A planning committee may have difficulty seeing the wisdom and necessity of this kind of celebration. One congregation in Ohio that hired a consultant to deal with the leaving of their minister ended up doing a series of skits under the umbrella title of "This is your life, George." In this humorous yet realistic approach, the congregation and pastor were able to recount their history together -- and celebrate both the good and the not so good of it.

Getting in Touch With Our Closure Style
All of us have predictable patterns of leave-taking. The pattern may vary slightly from time to time, but basically we have a similar routine we go through when we wish to say goodbye.

A quick insight into your exit style can occur if you reflect on the last social affair you were attending. Think back to the way you left the party. Be in touch with your feelings about yourself during the exit period. In microcosm you have a picture of your typical exit pattern.

For a deeper look at your exit style, think back to the first time you left your family (leaving for a week at camp; going away to college; getting married -- what-

ever). How did you gain closure with your family members before you left? Your recollection of that process will give you a clearer view of your termination style.

Diagramatically the process looks like this:

The normal assumption about disengagement is that it occurs gradually, as represented by the dotted line. In actual fact, our pattern of disengagement can best be characterized by a broken line, that has specific identifiable turning points on it. When placed together these turning points or bits of behavior constitute our termination style. In short, all of us go through a certain routine when saying "good-bye." That routine includes cliches, body movements, promises, questions, etc.

The following things can be said about this process:

a) Transitions are better characterized by a step process (as above) than a curved line. We should be able to identify the points of movement as well as the plateaus. (See above points of movement).

b) Each of us has a pattern of behavior as to how we engage in and disengage from relationships.

c) We will have an easier time changing the length of time within which we run our pattern than we will in changing the pattern itself. (We can either lengthen or shorten the time in which we run our pattern.) It will require something as dramatic as a serious crisis or intensive

*Coping With Stress and Transition, Charles Seashore, Ph.D., NTL Institute, Bethel, Maine, July 4-9, 1977.

therapy for us to change our pattern permanently.

d) We repeat our pattern in a twenty minute relationship on a bus or a twenty year marriage. As a tadpole recapitulates the history of millions of years of frog development, so I recapitulate my pattern of entering and exiting regardless of the nature or depth of the relationship.

The implications of this theory are mind-boggling. I have a set pattern of disengaging with people. I will run this pattern when

1) I say farewell to a casual acquaintance...

2) I say farewell to a very deep friendship...

3) I say farewell to a parish I've been serving for 5 years or more...

4) I say farewell to others at the time of my death.

This is my pattern of disengagement. This doesn't mean that I can't change it with some intentionality on my part. It does mean, however, that when I'm not intentional about doing it differently, I will revert to my same old pattern.

Before we begin planning our strategy for terminating with a parish, it would be helpful for us to be clearer about our typical way of disengaging. We may find there are some self-defeating aspects to our exit pattern.

A simple exercise with some friends will deliver some quick insight and feedback on your exit style. Invite three other people to join you around a table. The exercise is done non-verbally so no talking is allowed. All participants allow themselves to be represented by their right hand. Each person is to draw an imaginary arc in front of him/her which is to represent their private space. Whenever it suits them, people are to move beyond their private space and engage others through the use of their hands. They may touch, explore, hold, push, grip, etc. - whatever comes naturally as they engage each other in the center of the table. When it feels right, each person is to return to his/her own private space. People may retreat to their private space for a time and then move out to engage others again.

Once everyone is finished, take some time to reflect and share personal perceptions of self and others as to entry and exit patterns. More than likely everyone will recognize patterns of behavior that are typical of them as they move in and out of groups.

Take some time now to reflect on your exit style. Add to this the reflections on how you left your last social gathering and your perceptions of how you disengaged from your family as a younger person. All this should give you a good fix on your termination style.

What do you like about your pattern? What do you dislike about it? Is this the way you want to leave your parish? Is this the way you want to die? If not, what do you want to change about all that?

Modeling Closure for Our People

There are various ways of ministering to people. Guidance, instruction, exhortation are some examples. Another distinct method is that of modeling. Very few of us would ever have caught the faith had it not been for the people who modeled dimensions of spirituality for us.

This then may be our final act of ministry in a congregation. We may be able to model for them ways in which they can gain closure with significant others. Perhaps we can visualize a congregational member trying to cope with imminent death, being grateful to a pastor who taught him/her how to die by the manner in which the pastor left that parish.

We are able to serve as models as we get better at gaining meaningful closure with loved and not-so-loved parishioners. It is an art for which we've had little or no preparation. We need to gain the skill and insights needed in the absence of other good models around us. It must be done within the context of a "denial of death" society -- a culture which develops attitudes and practices which militate against effective closures. Out of our belief in the death-resurrection cycle of human life, we may learn to serve as models for others as we get better and better at starting up with people, becoming deeply involved with them, closing out with them, and starting anew with other people.

In order to be effective models for our members, however, our humanness should stand out much more predominately than our clergyness. In our call to wholeness, we have been called to be fully human -- nothing more, nothing less. It is death that reminds us what that's really all about. We are creatures; finite, mortal, limited. No matter how creative or profound we were in life, in death we share this one thing in common with the rest of the animal kingdom -- we die. Little wonder we curse death. It is the reminder of that aspect of our humanity.

To model effective closure involves being able to live deeply into the human side of death -- the death of relationships -- the death of roles and functions and responsibilities -- the death of that special relationship a pastor has with a parish.

At times we may discover ourselves having more difficulty letting go of the role we played with people than letting go of the people themselves. A symptom of this is the desire to maintain our role throughout the termination process. Dying to the parish involves dying to our role with people as well. Our failure to die to this role with congregational members gets us involved in pastoral acts with them long after we've left. Our hanging onto these roles is our bid for immortality. We allow ourselves to be indispensable with people, insuring our ability to live forever in their lives.

To model termination is to be able to let go -- and to be open and candid about the feelings that emerge in that letting go. In our modeling the "letting go" process, we also are able to help others gracefully let go of chunks of their lives in farewells and in death. Along the way we become better prepared for our own final stage of growth, our own death. The many farewells from congregations are preparatory courses for our final course -- learning how to die well.

The Positive Side of Things

In all this, it's easy to get into all the "oughts" of good terminations. It can become like other things we've learned in seminary or elsewhere.

Missing is the resurrection side of all these "death" experiences. Deep down we all know this -- that is, when we face in-

to our fears and anxieties and try to hang in there with honesty and candor about what's really going on with us -- that it always seems to come out the other end as a more wholesome, lifegiving experience. It's at those times that we really feel affirmed in our humanity. There is a freshness and meaning to life that we hadn't experienced before.

For me this is where Dr. Kubler-Ross makes her most profound point. Death can be the final stage of growth, depending on how we approach it. One way to approach it is to resist and avoid it.

The soul in torment is a person tortured from attachment to life, a torture which surges through our whole being, chilling us to our heart one minute and breaking us out in a flushing sweat the next. This is our frantic struggle to clutch at life while slipping over the brink of death. This is the self in battle with the non-self.

The alternate experience can be much like the story of Miss Martin in Mwalimu Imara's concluding article in Death, the Final Stage of Growth.

Miss Martin had been a holy terror when she came to the institute. All her life she had been a hard driving, joyless lady with few close friends. It was only through some intensive work by a committed staff that she was able to come to view herself in a different way. Near the time of her death, she was able to share in a death and dying seminar the following things:

I have lived more in the past three months than I have during my whole life... I wish I knew forty years ago what I know now about living. I have friends. Thank you.

Imara continues,

We cried. All of us. Nurses, social workers, ministers, physicians, all crying for that miracle that was Miss Martin. Here was a woman with tremendous will and presence who could still frighten people who crossed her. She had grown bitter in her ruthless encounter with the world of her experience, taking but unable to give or receive from anyone, that is until she met us. The miracle of Miss Martin was the transformation from a lifestyle of hardness to the open softness of the beautiful old woman before us at the seminars.

That, friends, is the quality of things we miss for ourselves when we try to run through the thistle patch. As painful as termination might be, we miss the opportunity to come to grips with our lives by looking at them from another perspective -- from the perspective of terminating relationships with friends and parishioners. I am firmly convinced that our termination experience while ending a ministry is the precursor of the way we will die. And if death is the final stage of growth, as I believe it is, then we can receive a downpayment on that growth by allowing our ministerial closures to be those kinds of life-enhancing, rich, joyful experiences. These are the events that can transform us -- if we are willing -- into the kind of down-to-earth, loving, human persons we really want to be. Beyond this, these events are able to greatly enhance the quality of our lives and our ministries. They are able to become the times at which, when looking back, we feel we have lived most fully.

Take it from an old thistle runner from way back. When I think back on my first termination experience with a parish, I realize that that's exactly what I did. I had had a real love affair with that congregation up in Kingston, Ontario. During my fifth year with them, I received an opportunity for a position in a line of ministry I had always hoped to get into: professional youth worker at a judicatory level (600 congregations). It absolutely tore me to shreds. My only way through it -- so it seems - was to keep a stiff upper lip and plough on through it. It took me three years of grieving before I could even do some honest reflecting on it.

I'm very clear at this point about how my inability to grieve with those people in an honest, open way led to some dysfunctional behavior in my new setting. My anger and my guilt got acted out in several inappropriate ways. That is another story, too long to tell here, but my friends and enemies in Central Pennsylvania, I'm certain, would agree with this perception.

Since that time, I believe I've learned something about termination styles. I knew there had to be a better way. My work with the whole human potential movement plus four years of therapy have helped me to be more in touch with my feelings as to express those feelings more openly. Terminations are not dreadful experiences for me anymore. I've really come to know firsthand what a rich, growing experience they can be. Even as I write this, I'm aware of termination coming up for me as I leave a metropolitan training center where I've been working for the last four and a half years. This side of that experience, it still frightens me. If I had my druthers, I'd just as soon "slip away into the night." But I now know what I'd be missing if I did it that way. It will be a time of surprises -- it always has been. It will be a time when I'll more clearly know and appreciate what I mean to people and what they mean to me. I know I will come away from that experience feeling different about all that than I do now.

Throughout all of this, it is our faith that gets the real workout. We are really best able to lean into the death experience of terminating a ministry when we live in grace. At some point in the process we need to simply let go and allow grace to carry us through the moment. Paul Tillich describes it so eloquently when he says,

Grace strikes us when we are in great pain and restlessness. It strikes us when we walk through the dark valley of a meaningless and empty life. It strikes us when we feel that our separation is deeper than usual, because we have violated another life, a life which we loved, or from which we were estranged. It strikes us when our disgust for our own being, our indifference, our weakness, our hostility, our lack of direction and composure have become intolerable to us. It strikes us when year after year the longed for perfection of life does not appear, when the old compulsions reign within us as they have for decades, when despair destroys all joy and courage. Sometimes at that moment a wave of light breaks into our darkness, and it is as though a voice were saying: "You are accepted. You are accepted, accepted by that which is greater than you, and the name of which you do not know. Do not ask for the name now; perhaps you

*will find it later. Do not try to do any-
thing now; perhaps later you will do much.
Do not seek for anything; do not perform
anything; do not intend anything.* Simply
accept the fact that you are accepted!" 1.

Going through the grief process of terminating a ministry can move us toward a
blessed "acceptance." But the steps lead-
ing to this kind of acceptance feel as
though they move through the "valley of
the shadow of death." They may require
of us what our ministries have not asked
of us up 'till this point. Dr. Imara de-
signed and executed a research project,
hoping to gain an understanding of the
religious dynamics behind the denial process and the terminally ill patients' re-
sistance to moving through to acceptance.
His experiment demonstrated that people
who deny less and are able to move more
easily through the grief process are
those who:

1) are willing to converse in depth
with significant others about what their
present experience is like,

2) meet others on equal terms, that is,
are able to enter into real dialogue with
others, and

3) accept the good with the bad. They
have a framework within which the tragic
and happy events of their present and
past life take on meaning and give their
life a sense of direction and fulfillment.

Those three qualities appear to me to
fit together into a healthy working model
for closing out a ministry. The ability
to execute all three may not come to us
overnight, but they are skills and attitudes that we can work at and become better
at. With the termination of ministries
yet to come, perhaps we will be able to
execute them well at the time of our own
death.

One thing I'm clear about. I don't
want to use the thistle patch approach
when I leave this world. I really would
like it to be my final stage of growth.

Come join me in the venture.

1. Paul Tillich, The Shaking of the Found-
ations, New York, Charles Scribner's Sons,
1948, p. 162.

A Psychological Postscript

This past summer I had the opportunity to
share some of my theories on termination
and start up with a friend of mine, John
Hughes, a psychologist, who works for the
Fife Regional Council in England as an
Area Social Work Organizer. I shared
with him my discovery that most of us have
very predictable patterns of entering
into and exiting from relationships with
other people. John indicated that his experiences in counseling would verify that
conclusion. "In fact," he said, "I believe it goes even deeper. I contend
that saying "Hello" and saying "Good-bye"
are the two major learning tasks all hu-
mans need to accomplish." John continued,
"I would venture to say that 98% of all
the people in Institutions for the Emotionally Disturbed are there because they
fouled up at either saying 'Hello' or saying 'Good-bye.' Some children come into this world and have no one in their
family really say 'Hello' to them. Can
you imagine what it's like trying to learn
to say 'Hello' to others in the world,
when no one ever said 'Hello' to you when
you were born?"

Some morning in September go to a grade
school and watch first graders try to
say "Hello" to each other that first day
of school. Some do O.K., but others never
seem to get it right. Some young boy de-
cides to say "Hello" by taking another
child's toy away from him.

Others never learn to say "Good-bye."
Some have never said "Good-bye" to Mamma
or Daddy! Hence, even though he or she
has long since passed on, he or she still
continues to dominate this person's life.
Some have been jilted in love and yet
never say "good-bye" to that relationship.
As a result, they carry that failure into
subsequent relationships.

Most of us could use some continued work
on saying "Good-bye" and "Hello." One
way we can monitor our personal psychological health is by taking time to critique
once again the manner in which we say
"Hello" and "Good-bye." By adopting some
simple disciplines like keeping a diary or
doing some journal keeping throughout our
transition, we can try to become somewhat
objective about our style of saying "hello" and "good-bye." In the process we

will learn a good deal about ourselves. These insights will probably determine the learning goals we set for ourselves in the future. Some could conceivably involve some continued work with a therapist.

If nothing else, I do hope the sharing of this psychological perspective will give you some sense of adventure at learning new things about yourself as you move into your next transition. I see it as congruent with the theological perspective on transitions that I shared with you earlier.

APPENDIX A: A Case in Point
The following conversation was recorded on tape March 5, 1976.

George and Ted were reviewing George's termination from his parish in Ohio. Ted had a contract to do a specific piece of work in the parish, hence his presence there at the time of George's resignation. Instead, Ted did some great work as a mid-wife, assisting George and the parish to live into the grief that was theirs.

I believe the conversation to be significant for a host of reasons.

(1) It illustrates in specific detail the Kubler-Ross stages of grief as experienced by a parish and its pastor: denial, bargaining, anger, guilt, acceptance.

I am particularly impressed with the dynamic of denial. It was present in Ted. It was present in George. The Vestry was using it to cope the evening of George's resignation. The interview points out vividly how denial and avoidance can be expected everywhere at the time of termination.

(2) It illustrates how insight into these stages of grief can assist people to understand the behavior people exhibit when a pastor is leaving a parish.

(3) It articulates graphically the relationship between transition, grief, and stress. George had probably surpassed his threshold level of stress and was somewhat dysfunctional until he owned up to his own grief at leaving and allowed himself to feel it completely.

(4) The interview introduces a new dynamic - namely that often the grief of the pastor is over things not accomplished. A big part of George's grief was in admitting to "things unfinished." When he finally was able to give these up, his stress level decreased significantly.

(5) The interview gets at the power dynamics and the power shifts that occur when a pastor resigns. The "outs" wake up and sniff the air. Changes are coming!

(6) The Farewell Breakfast sounds like a neat termination event. It had the note of reality to it - including the negative aspects of George's ministry as well as the positive. It confirmed for me the value of having a consultant present assisting parishioners to plan for such an event.

(7) The conversation also surfaces the kind of symbolism that emerges as people deal with the departing clergy. They illustrate the deep and complex ties people have with their pastor. In this interview the symbols of "divorce" and "widow" are examples.

(8) Finally, the conversation around the leased car is significant. I'm impressed by Ted's insight into what that symbolized for some folks.

Conversation between George Reynolds and Ted Blumenstein on the subject of Termination of the Rector-Parish Relationship on March 5, 1976
George had left the parish December 31, 1975; Ted had served as Associate Rector from September 1, 1975 and as Interim Rector from January 1, 1976.

George: It might be useful to try to do a recollection and look back to the early days, when you knew that I was going to Minneapolis for job interviews and virtually nobody else knew that.

Ted: The first thing that I remember from that time is the ambivalence inside of myself. After you made the decision that you would like to have that position, my head told me that it was right for you. And from what I had observed from working around here for three months, I knew that what you had done here was a completed piece of work that was irreversible. Things here were healthy and it was a good time for you to move. But I still never lost the hope that we were going to complete our scheme of working nine months together. The ambivalence was in me right from the beginning and it heightened as the time approached for you to leave.

George: I think for the record we need to say that we had just worked out a set of goals for the next nine months and that we were both turned on by them. That was the thing that you say that you had a hard time letting go, even though you saw the desire to leave in me.

Ted: Right. We started pursuing the nine month goals on September 1. Your resignation came October 20.

George: We were only two months into it.

Ted: And we were feeling good about how we were pursuing the goals.

George: Yes, we were both turned on by that. I was able to let go of those goals first. I perceived the incongruence of our conversations sooner than you did. We would sit down to talk, and you especially would talk in terms of continuing to work on those goals. I was doing it also, to some extent. But I think I was seeing the end quicker than you were. By that time, I had told the other parish that I was coming.

Ted: As I recall, on two or three occasions I asked you to work with me on something. We got together but couldn't do it. Instead, we spent those meetings planning the termination process.

George: But our stated agenda had been to work on the goals.

Ted: And each of those times we rescheduled our work, and justified how we had spent our time. We needed to work on the termination process. We could work on the goals next week. This occurred several times.

George: The thing finally turned when we began to talk about grief, the stages of grief, and the grief process. In planning termination, we began to look at the fact that you in particular, and both of us to some extent, were denying the termination of our relationship as a team.

Ted: Right.

George: The concept of denial helped us realize what we were doing and realize that we weren't going to defeat nor avoid some natural dynamics.

Ted: I remember one time in November when you identified denial working in me before I was aware of it. And when you identified it I could see it clearly. Then within two days I got you back.

George: Yes, I remember that. I don't remember exactly how, but I remember the feeling.

Ted: At that point I really valued our team relationship for working on the termination. I got to thinking, "How long would it have taken me to understand that dynamic in myself without your help?" And I also felt helpful to you.

George: One of my main memories from that mid-November and early December is my own feeling of depression. First I had a sense of high -- feeling good about getting the call to a position I wanted. And the high of announcing it and getting appreciation from people -- the feeling of being appreciated. Then for several weeks came what I can only describe as the depression part of the grief process. Now I identify it as a part of the grief process. I had a hard time working (I had been working hard before that). I got into a mood where I had a hard time getting anything done, and there was a lot to do.

Ted: And the dizziness of Sunday morning.

George: Right. I was feeling faint on Sunday morning, as I shared with you. Actually every morning I was feeling okay at the start of the morning and very tired in the late morning. To the point where I had to go back to bed. I went to the doctor about it. By that time he knew I was leaving. He said that it must be a stressful period for me. He was the one who helped me see that the physical reactions were caused by stress. He gave me some tranquilizers and told me to get off coffee. With the medicine and with no coffee, I was OK within a week. Also the identification of what was causing the depression helped me. At first I denied it. I told the doctor that he wasn't right. Barbara said that I told her the same thing. Then I began to admit it.

Ted: And then you didn't have to worry about a physical illness. You got rid of that worry.

George: I admitted to myself that I was under a lot of stress. I began to analyze it with your help and Barbara's help. Maybe analyzing it was what relieved me. I had come here to this parish with very high hopes. It is part of me to have really extremely high expectations -- unreal expectations -- of what I want to accomplish: visions of this parish very much oriented to the community.

Ted: Wasn't a Regional Education and Training Center a part of the vision?

George: Yes. That was not a realistic thing. That was a part of the dream. Even though I saw them as unrealistic, they were a part of my gut expectations that I never gave up until I said I was leaving. And that was my grief.

Ted: Time had always been on your side.

George: Yes. It was always to be done in the future. Once I said I was leaving, I had to give up those expectations.

Ted: I saw that being acted out at your last Vestry meeting. You made a final report to the Vestry and you wrote a farewell letter to the congregation. Do you remember the nature of those two things? The farewell letter to the congregation made very positive statements about your views of this parish now and in the future. Your report to the Vestry was the things you were just discussing. "Things Unfinished" was the title of it. That was the letting go. It wasn't appropriate to write that to everybody, so you chose to say it to the Vestry.

George: Identifying that I was giving them up, that I was leaving them, cured me of my physical disabilities. I had to have help from the doctor for the stress, but once I started admitting that, I could let go of it and be free. I got over the depression. I've got another word -- word for the whole process -- it's the word sadness. It's crying about it, being openly sad. I don't know that I had shed tears in November, but I let myself feel the sadness of not doing all the things I had planned.

Ted: There are ways of crying other than with tears. For instance, with your dizziness.

George: Yes, that's right. I think sadness and acceptance are very much bound up with each other. Open grief puts you out of the depression and into acceptance.

Ted: I was more aware of what other people in the parish had to do. Handling anger is the one I noticed the most.

George: Let's go back and look at the parish's grief process.

Ted: And more of your stuff might come up while we're doing it.

George: In this conversation I started with me. Actually, last fall, when you and I were talking about the grief process, we did all our thinking in terms of the parish grief process. It was only much later that I realized that I was going through a grief process. So our discussion now is out of order. First we began to see things in the parish.

Ted: For the record we should say that we made a conscious decision to use the grief process with the Kubler-Ross terminology for our own understanding of the behavior we were seeing in the parishioners It helped us to understand what was going on and helped us to make appropriate responses. We didn't plan any interventions to help people express anger, but I was aware that I was helping people identify the anger that they were feeling. My intervention was to make it more explicit. Let me tell this antecdote about Jim Brown. He came to me to tell me how he responded to the news that you were leaving. Since you knew that he was very fond of you, and that it was going to be hard, you gave him personal notification. You went to see him. Did he ever tell you what happened? Mark knew that you had gone to tell him, and Mark was also aware that this could be hard for Jim to accept. After you left Jim's house, Mark called him and said "How are you doing?" Jim said "Oh, just fine, George was just here to see me." Then he broke into tears. Mark then went to Jim and spent the major part of the afternoon with him.

George: I didn't know that.

Ted: When Jim reported this to me, he told me that Mark had helped him to see that what he had gained from you was not going to be destroyed because of your leaving. The growth he had in the last seven years was his. While he and I were talking I pointed out the anger that he had toward you for leaving. At that point he owned it, but said he had not been aware of it before.

George: He could not realize how angry he is. He really does love me.

Ted: I saw the bargaining stage of the Kubler-Ross model in the conversation between Mark and Jim. We're not giving it up. It's not going to be all that different. He can physically leave but what he offers you, you'll still have. And then I came along and pointed out something else in his description - the anger. So we were really using the model.

George: The model helped me in the Vestry meeting. I called a special session to announce my resignation to the Vestry before I announced it to the congregation. I had a prepared statement that I read. There was a stunned silence from the Vestry, which I interpreted as a kind of denial. It was partly denial and partly anger.

Ted: Yes, I was hearing the anger.

George: The first thing they said was "Just like that, is that all there is to it?" then, "I'm not surprised."

Ted: The anger was more in the manner of saying it than in the words.

George: Yes. The anger was there. The 10 women were the only ones who knew ahead of time and they did most of the talking. The women started talking with each other about making arrangements for a Search Committee, how they would go about getting one. It sort of felt like the relatives coming in and making arrangements for a funeral. The arrangements -- how they would go about getting another rector, seeing the bishop -- all the continuity symbols.

Ted: Becky reported to me that she felt very good about things the next time I saw her. As incoming Senior Warden she was going to make sure that things happened properly during this period. She had already appointed Howard to chair the Search Committee. She was already thinking into January, making plans for the continuity.

George: For the 10 women, at this point, continuity was a big thing. I think I would have had a hard time at that meeting if I had not read my resignation letter. I was having a hard time understanding the way people were behaving.

Ted: No expression of sorrow and no well-wishing.

George: The concept of denial and the concept of anger enabled me to deal with the meeting. Otherwise, I would have just felt vacant; but I didn't because I was processing it through those concepts. Those are my main memories.

Ted: I'm wondering if because the 10 women knew about the resignation in advance that they might have been farther along in the termination process. Maybe they had already touched base with those initial feelings of denial and anger. They were at a different stage than the Vestry.

George: Well Howard, as Senior Warden, had known I was in negotiations with the parish for several months. And Becky, the Junior Warden, had known even longer that this parish was interested in me. When I told Becky a month before, there was real shock on her part. So she had gotten over that.

Ted: This is not to say that we don't all recycle those initial reactions. The two Wardens had the news first, and so they were able to do something else.

Let's now talk about Bruce at the last Vestry meeting. You had finished your farewell report, and you were leaving the room because the Vestry was going to talk about a farewell dinner. Do you remember what happened as you were walking out of the room?

George: No, what happened?

Ted: Bruce swung at you with his fist, playfully, and said, "All you told us are the things you didn't get done." I saw him swinging at you with his fist. I'm certain that he would describe it as a gentle pat.

I'd like to record some things that you discovered from some brief encounters. After the meeting we've been talking about, the resignation letter went out to the parish. By the next time people saw you, they had read the letter. Didn't you say that you had some brief encounters, like Sunday morning at the door of the church, in which people showed where they were in terms of the termination process? You expressed that elderly people seemed to reach acceptance faster than younger people.

George: Right. It was as if they had gone through all the stages of the process. I talked to Mary about leaving. She expressed disappointment, regret, and grief. The thing I saw in her and in several other older people was that they had gone through grief so often, they had lost so many friends, children, husbands, and so forth, that they were practiced. They are skillful at it. They can let themselves go through this process knowing that there is an end to it and a new life ahead. The older people, who are mature, showed that they knew how to deal with it. People my age were having a much harder time -- the things with Jim and with Bruce are examples.

Ted: Let me bring in another person who is very close to you -- Henry. Because he was working on the Farewell Breakfast, he and I got into conversation about what we were celebrating. I shared with him the way you and I had been using the termination process for understanding what was going on. That evoked from him his denial. He told me that for other people it will be the closing of the relationship with you. But not for him because he'll come to see you in Minnesota. He'll spend his vacations with you. He has plans for how he is going to keep the relationship alive.

George: That's a good example. When I first told Jim that I was leaving one of the first things he said was, "Will you come back here and do a wedding?" -- he was thinking about Susie's wedding. And I said "No." That really did it.

Ted: That is a symbolic question. It's not as though the wedding were planned for this spring. It's probably ten years off.

George: Yes, it's obviously a symbolic question, and I had presence enough to say no because I knew how much harm I could do. I really don't like those weddings by former Rectors.

Ted: Let's turn to the Farewell Breakfast and the preparation that went into it.

George: The Farewell Breakfast was a joyful funeral service.

Ted: It started when I called together a group of people who knew the history of your seven years here. Part of the grief process is the recalling of the history of the relationship. These folks met and quickly put onto newsprint the traumatic occurences of the seven years, like the by-laws fight and the Black Manifesto. Then we turned to the positive and wrote the slogans they have heard you use about the ideal parish. When they worked all of that into a presentation it came through to you as positive but without denying the negative.

George: It was a very humorous approach to the negative, and the positive, both.

Ted: And the people at the breakfast who knew you well were laughing and crying at the same time.

George: You saw that better than I did. I was rather overcome.

Ted: At about that time people were beginning to show more interest in where you were going and what kind of parish you were going to. This topic had become a thing of interest in the informal communication of the parish. Mark had picked it up at parties and brought it to the December staff meeting. People were fantasizing about this huge place in Minnesota.

George: Going back to the Farewell Breakfast, we had a description of it. It was a huge feast, with lots of dancing and fun. It was like a widow recalling the

events of the marriage relationship as a way of coping with grief.

Ted: Just the way the person who has lost a spouse gives a lot of thought to how they met and courted. The skit gave a lot of thought to how you were called to the parish and the early days.

George: Then there were also the people who were glad to see me go.

Ted: Yes. Did you say they were more apt to ask about the place where you were going?

George: Yes, as they made polite conversation. I really heard very little from them.

Ted: People who had not used their influence in the parish for years came out of the woodwork and were pushing for the formation of the Search Committee. The formation of that committee was difficult. Howard wanted the perfect committee that would be acclaimed by the whole parish. He was getting a lot of pressure put on him for it to be a conservative group. There were debates among the people about the advisability of reversing the clock and going back seven years. Others were saying that that's impossible.

George: I kind of had a feeling that all of that was going on. The problem was that those people were in power with Sam (the former Rector) and out of power with me. They really were. They withdrew from the church except for token membership, as a consequence of feeling out of power. So when I left they moved in at a point where they could exercise power.

Ted: The first thing they did was to tie up Howard for a month. He was so reluctant to move. When finally he had to put together a Search Committee, he wanted some people on it who had not been active for five years or more. He had a devil of a time. They were using their influence at the informal level, but did not want to be on the committee. I heard he went to four people before he got someone from that drop-out group.

George: Our time is about up. Have we covered the essentials?

Ted: Well, we covered the announcement of resignation, the reaction to it, the Farewell Breakfast, and putting together the Search Committee. Then some things of interest happened after you left. Requiring you to pay rent on the parish car, even though it was not being used, was

like the petty details in a divorce set-
tlement. I think a lot of the anger was
being acted out through that car.

There was a lot of fantasy about how
long you kept a secret. Some thought that
surely you knew you were leaving when you
took the four month sabbatical in 1974 -
or when you had me come as Associate.
"What kind of thing was he pulling on us?"
was one angry expression. Some people re-
fused to accept that you did not know you
were leaving until right before you announced it. They wanted to believe that
there had been a conspiracy.

George: I did not hear it until after
I left.

APPENDIX B

Liturgies and Rituals
The Western church has so avoided the
reality of clergy/congregation termination
that very few rituals or liturgies have
been written to give expression to the deep
feelings persons have at those times.
Meaningful liturgies really should take
what is powerful and real in our lives and
give them perspective
-- ground them in good theology
-- lift them up to God in praise and
thanksgiving.

In my experience this has not really
happened in a creative helpful way at the
times when clergy leave their parishes.

We have installation services galore.
Why aren't there more services of departure and farewell?

I would encourage the writing and sharing of more of these in the future. Perhaps the Alban Institute could be the ve-
hicle for the sharing of them. Do let us
hear from you if you know of such liturgies
or rituals. Two liturgies come to mind
for the present. The first is written in
a book entitled Ritual in a New Day: An
Invitation (Abingdon, 1976). The book con-
tains a specific liturgy for the leave-
taking of a clergyperson.

The second was shared with me by my
friend Leon Hopper. It is really an installation service, but occurred in the
congregation he had left, where he was invited back to participate. I found it to
be a meaningful liturgical piece which
gave expression to the deeper feelings of
both the new minister and the departing
minister. Dr. Vigor is the president of

the congregation calling the new minister.
Dr. Haslund is the president of the congregation the new minister has just left.
Leon Hopper is the former minister who has
just left.

Dr. Vigor: Lex, we called you here
from far off to be minister of our church.
We called you because we felt a sense of
promise in what we might come to mean to
each other.

The Minister: I'm glad you called me,
because I too felt this sense of promise.
I liked the people here immediately, liked
looking forward to living among you.

Dr. Haslund: It was hard for us in
Santa Barbara to say goodbye, after so many
years of being with you. You had shared
a lot of living with us, lived through
ever so many crises and triumphs with us.
You became part of us. We are still
grieving at the loss; but, at the same
time, we have begun to feel the promise
of a new kind of life that is emerging.

The Minister: I too, of course, experience the grief, the pain of parting, of
being separated from people I love.

Rev. Hopper: My own life has been in-
tertwined with the lives, the being of
the people here in much the same way yours
was with the people of the Santa Barbara
church. These people are part of who I
now am. It is my hope that you will give
them the best that is in you, that you will
care deeply about their well-being and your
own. It is my hope that your life with
these good people will prove to be as re-
warding as mine has been.

Dr. Vigor: Leon, we miss you. You were
here when we were born, helped us grow up.

The Minister: I am aware of your presence on every hand as I move about in the
church, in the community. You are still
here. And it is clearly a vibrant, vital
institution you helped our people to create.

The Congregation: Lex, we affirm you
as our new minister: we want you to move
among us, be with us, share with us in
the quest for a life that is rich, full,
abundant, complete. Together we will find
our way.

The Minister: I rejoice in that af-
firmation, and will give the best that is
in me to performing the tasks, to meeting
the responsibilities implicit in it. Together we will discover what it means to
be human, to be alive in this place, in
this time.